CW00567589

4

Sandlings Walks
II: Orford to Dunwich

15 Circular Walks from Orford to Dunwich

Geoff Gostling

ISBN 0-9525478-3-X

Printed by Portman Press
Published by G J Gostling
Copyright © G J Gostling

Cover Picture: Iken Church and the Alde

CONTENTS

Foreword   3

Introduction   4

About the Area   4

Walks

Foreword

Micro Ramblers are highly localised walk books. Each book in the series contains 15 walks in a comparatively small area. These are almost always circular, and often linked so that two or more may be joined to form longer walks if required.

Instructions for each individual walk are contained on the right-hand page, with the relevant map on the left, so there's no need to turn over pages while you're walking (unless you're joining 2 or more together).

The average length is between 7km and 8km (4½-5 miles). The scale of sketch maps is usually about 4cm to 1km or 2½in to 1 mile.

All walks use rights of way, permissive paths or unclassified roads. Limited use is made of main roads for joining paths or getting to and from car parks.

Right of way means you have a right of passage, but no right to stray from the path. You also have a right to expect that paths be unobstructed; farmers should reinstate paths within 2 weeks of ploughing if weather permits.

Distances are given in metres and kilometres. If you're more at home with yards and miles, it may be of help to remember that 1 yard is about 1 metre, 800 metres is a half-mile, 1½km is about 1 mile. Times are based on average walking speeds. As a rough guide, at an average walking speed, it takes about 12 minutes to walk 1km, or just over 1 minute to walk 100m.

Bus routes are supplied where applicable, but please check routes and times with Eastern Counties.

Please remember the Country Code. Machinery, livestock and crops are the farmers livelihood. Help them, and help preserve wildlife by observing a few simple rules:

Guard against risk of fire;	Take litter home
Protect wildlife plants & trees;	Use gates & stiles to cross fences;
Fasten gates;	Leave livestock alone;
Keep pets under control;	Don't pollute water;
Keep to rights of way;	Don't make unnecessary noise;

Introduction

This is the second of the Sandlings Walks books in the Micro Rambler series. Book I explored the southern area, from Sutton Hoo to Orford. Book II continues with a variety of walks from Orford as far as Dunwich.

As in book I, the variety includes heathland, forests, small villages, river banks and sea shore. Please note that, although the forest walks mainly use public rights of way, some forest tracks which aren't rights of way are also used. Forest Enterprise welcomes walkers on most of the forest tracks, but reserve the right to close them from time to time. If you do find a track closed, there is usually a viable alternative without taking you too much out of the way.

Walks 3, 4 and 15 involve some river bank or beach walking. At normal high tides these should present no problem, but at spring tides the paths may be covered. If you find this is the case, either take an alternative route back if available, or wait a few minutes for the tide to drop.

All walks are contained in Landranger Sheet 156 (except a very small part of Walk 1). You may find this sheet useful in getting to start points. (Grid references are provided in the heading information for each walk). If you haven't got Landranger 156, the outline map on page 36 should help.

Please note that forest walks, by their very nature, are difficult to describe when referring to footpaths. Trees are about the least permanent items in a forest. It's not much good describing a change of direction as being near a tree if the tree disappears the following week!

For this reason, description of routes in forests lean quite heavily on distances to be covered, which are fairly accurate, and the quality of the path, e.g. stony, grassy etc. Please pay particular attention to these. The forests are quite large, and, if you miss a turning, you could go well out of your way before noticing anything wrong. A compass would also be of help in checking your direction against the maps in the book.

About the Area

Aldeburgh: A small seaside town with lots of character. Benjamin Britten and Peter Pears lived here, and lie in the local parish churchyard of Saints Peter and Paul, along with other eminent musicians. They helped to make Aldeburgh famous for music festivals. There are a lot of interesting listed buildings, but the Moot Hall is probably the best known and most photographed.

Aldringham: A heathland village, originally known as Aldringham-cum-Thorpe. (Thorpe became Thorpeness). There's a small church next to a set of 19th century almshouses (Ogilvie Almshouses). There's also a good pub called the Parrot and Punchbowl.

Dunwich: In King John's day, it was only slightly smaller than Ipswich, with 9 churches and 2 monasteries. Most of it now lies under the sea and not one of the original churches remains. Now there's a few houses, a good museum, the excellent Ship pub, a fish and chip shop, and the gateway to Greyfriars Priory.

Eastbridge: A small village near Minsmere Nature Reserve. There's a good village pub, the Eels Foot.

Friston: A small village with one of the largest post mills in Suffolk, regrettably lacking sails. There's a good pub, the Old Chequers.

Iken: A somewhat mysterious village, with St Botolphs church standing in apparent isolation on a promontory above the river Alde. It may have been built on the site of St Botolph's Abbey, a place of pilgrimage then and now.

Leiston: A small town that grew with Richard Garrett's ironworks - now a splendid museum. There's an impressive ruined abbey just north of the town.

Orford: A lovely village - there's a Norman Keep, a fine church with a ruined Norman chancel, 2 good pubs, a hotel, gift shops, and a good smokehouse.

Snape: Most people have heard of Snape Maltings, internationally famous as a concert hall, but there are other things to see as well, such as a variety of shops and the Plough and Sail pub. The village itself has several interesting features - go and see the church on the Aldeburgh road. There was a ship burial too, similar to the one at Sutton Hoo, discovered in 1862 on Church Common.

Sudbourne: Small village on the edge of the forest. The pub has been converted to a private house, sad to say. The attractive small church, with its 'spirelet' is well out of the main village.

Thorpeness: Once the partner of Aldringham-cum-Thorpe, this became a popular holiday resort with the excavation of the Meare in 1910. There's one pub, the Dolphin (badly damaged by fire in 1995). It's also well known for an attractive post mill, and the House in the Clouds, a disguised water tower.

Westleton: Pleasant heathland village, with two pubs, a green and a duckpond. There are plenty of good walks on the heath.

WALK 1

This Walk →– –→ →·····→ →– –→
Roads
Other Paths/Walks ················

Start at (A)

Scale
1 KM
½ MILE

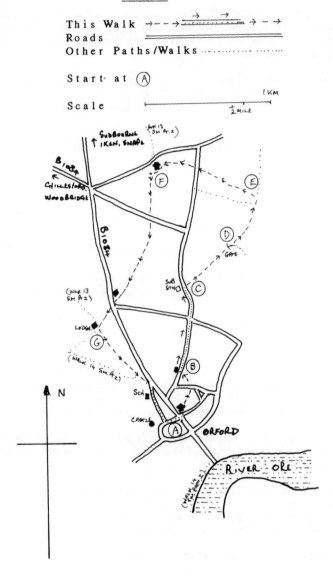

Walk 1

Distance: 5½km (3½m) 1-1½ hours
Start Point: Market Hill, Orford (GR 421499)
Route: Orford, Sudbourne Church
Pub: Kings Head, Orford
Car Parking: Market Hill
Bus Routes: 122, 160, 180, 636

A: Leave Market Hill towards the church.. Go into the churchyard by the gate next to the Kings Head. Walk past the church into the opposite corner. Follow the wall round into a lane, and along to a road.

B: Go straight across the road onto another footpath. Follow the path across the corner of a field towards a white house. Turn right when you reach the narrow road, and continue along for about 600m.

C: Just after a slight left hand bend, next to an electricity sub-station, turn right on a signed path across the field. Walk along parallel to the field edge about 40m to your left, to join it at a corner in about 200m. Continue along the field edge, to reach a gate in about 250m.

D: After the gate, turn right, then almost immediately left into a lane. In about 200m you'll see a signposted lane going up to the left. Go past this and continue on for another 50m, to find another signed path to the left

E: Here turn left across a field to a hedge in the far corner. *If the path isn't 'walkable', go along the lane for another 50m and turn left up a sandy track to reach the hedge. (Not a right of way, but it seems to be in common use).* Walk along the hedge and turn left on a signed path up the field. At the road cross onto a signed path towards some trees, concealing Sudbourne church. At the corner, walk along the field edge with a garden on your right. After passing the church you'll find a cross-path.

F: Turn left on the path. In 400m, cross a road and go on for 800m to reach the Orford road next to a bungalow. Go straight across, and walk along for about 250m to reach an unusual lodge on the right hand side.

G: Here, turn left on a good track. When you reach the Orford village sign, take the right fork to bring you out at the Castle end of Market Hill.

7

WALK 2

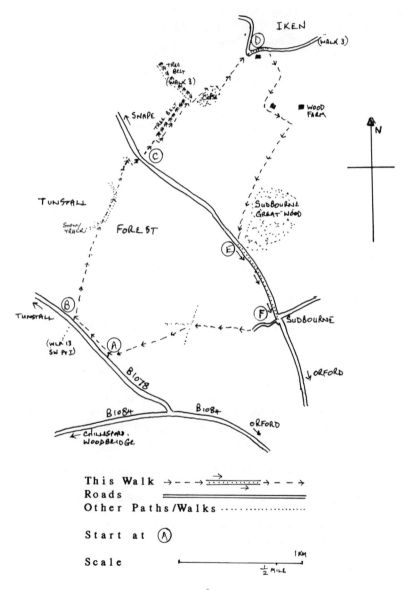

This Walk → - - → ⟶ ············ → - - →
Roads ══════════
Other Paths/Walks ····················

Start at Ⓐ

Scale |—————————————| 1 KM
                  ½ MILE

8

Walk 2

Distance: 8km (5m) 1½-2 hours
Start Point: Tunstall Forest (GR 399528)
Route: Tunstall Forest, Iken
Pub: No
Car Parking: Entrance to forest ride, ½ mile (800m) on the right hand
    side of the B1078, approaching from the B1084 Orford road..
Bus Routes: 122, 160, 180, 636 (B1084 only)

A: Please leave the forest ride access clear when you park the car. Go through the gate and almost immediately turn left on a Forestry track (Not a right of way), parallel to the road. In about 800m you'll reach a cross track, with a footpath entering the forest from the road on your left.

B: Turn right on the signed path into the forest. Keep more or less straight on for about 700m to join a stony forest track entering from your left. Continue on this for about 250m, and, where it swings left, go straight on along a pleasant path through young woodland. In about 200m follow it round to the right, then left again to bring you to a road.

C: Go across the road onto a signed path. Follow this field edge track for 700m to reach a wide cross track, with a small wood on the right. Go more or less straight on through the gateway and walk along with the wood on your right. In 200m, follow the track as it bends right round the edge of the wood, then shortly afterwards turn left on a signed path, with a thin line of silver birch on your right. Go straight on towards a cream coloured cottage, to emerge on a road on a corner.

D: Keep right at the road. About 100m after a pink washed thatched cottage, turn right on a concrete road. Stay on this for 900m to reach a T-junction, with Wood Farm clearly signed on the left. Here turn right on a signed track, and stay on it for about 1km to reach the Sudbourne road.

E: Turn left on the road, and follow it for about 700m down to the crossroads in Sudbourne.

F: Turn right into Blacklands Lane. In about 250m keep straight on into the forest. In about 500m at the bottom of a slight hill, you'll reach the intersection of several tracks. Here go half left on a wide stony track, to bring you back to your car in about 800m.

WALK 3

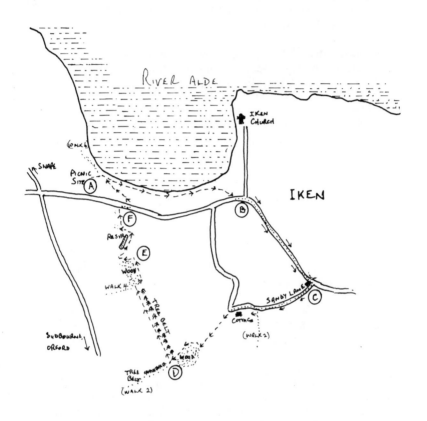

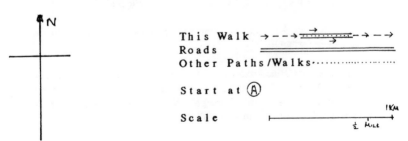

This Walk →–→ ·····→ →–→

Roads ═══════

Other Paths/Walks ···················

Start at Ⓐ

Scale ⊢————————————⊣ 1KM

½ MILE

10

Walk 3

Distance: 5½km (3½m) 1-1½ hours (6½km inc. St Botolph's church)
Start Point: Picnic Site, Iken (GR 400563)
Route: Iken Cliff, St Botolph's church, (Optional)
Pub: no
Car Parking: As above
Bus Routes: 160, 180

A: Leave the picnic site by the path in the bottom right hand corner.
Where the paths cross, take the one left of the cottage towards the shore.
In about 800m the path gradually leaves the shore, over some wooden
steps, to emerge on a narrow road.

B: Turn left on the road. *If you want to visit St. Botolph's church it's
about 550m down the narrow lane when you reach the bend - you'll have
to return the same way.* Otherwise continue on the road round the right
hand bend. Stay on this road for about 900m as far as Sandy Lane.

C: Turn right into Sandy Lane. In about 800m, at a sharp bend to the
right, continue on along a sandy track. Keep more or less straight on for
about 300m, following a thin line of silver birch, then turn right on a track
alongside a small wood. Stay on the track along the edge of the wood
when it bends left, and continue to a gateway in about 200m.

D: After passing through the gateway, turn right on a wide track with a
tree belt on your right hand side. When you get to the T-junction at the
end, turn right briefly then left on a wide track with a wood on your left.

E: In about 250m, continue following the edge of the wood as it bends
sharp left. The path heads slightly downhill for about 200m, then bends
right along the edge of a deep reservoir hidden in trees. In about 250m
you'll reach the head of the reservoir, where you should turn left on a
metalled farm road.

F: About 50m after joining the road cross a stile into the field on the right.
Head uphill towards the top left hand corner of the field, to reach a stile
onto a narrow road. Turn right on the road for 100m, then turn sharp left
on a signed track. Follow this track more or less straight on to bring you
back to the bottom of the picnic site.

11

WALK 4

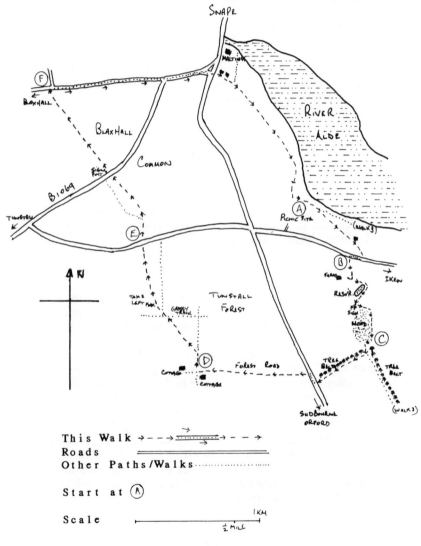

This Walk →– –→ →– –→
Roads
Other Paths/Walks ....

Start at Ⓐ

Scale |————————| 1 KM
      ½ MILE

12

Walk 4

Distance: 9½km (6m) 2-2½ hours
Start Point: Picnic Site, Iken (GR 400563)
Route: Tunstall Forest, Snape Maltings
Pub: Plough and Sail, Snape
Car Parking: As above
Bus Routes: 160, 180

A: Leave the picnic site by the path in the bottom right hand corner. Where the paths cross, take the signed path, slightly uphill, straight ahead. In about 400m you'll reach the road.

B: Turn right for 100m then cross a stile into a field on the left. Aim slightly left to cross a stile at the bottom and turn left on a farm road. After passing the head of a reservoir in about 50m, turn sharp right up the field/reservoir edge. When you reach the corner at the top follow the FP sign to the left. At the next corner turn right on the wide sandy track along the edge of the wood. Continue for 300m to a gap on the right.

C: At the gap, turn right, left and right again, so that you're walking along at a right angle to your original course with a tree belt on your right. In 500m turn briefly right on a road, then left on a wide forest track. Follow this for about 800m.

D: At a cross-ways, after a garden fence on the left, before a red-brick cottage on the right, turn right on a stony track. In 150m, where the track bends right, go more or less straight on along a grassy track. In 400m, cross another grassy track, and in another 75m at an apparent narrow fork take the left branch. In about 500m you'll reach a narrow road.

E: Go straight across the road on a broad ride. Ignore the inviting path between posts in 300m and stay on the main path for about another 400m to reach the Tunstall/Snape road. Go straight across on the signed path opposite. Keep straight on to reach the Snape/Blaxhall road in 1km.

F: Turn right on the road to reach Snape in about 1½km. Just before the Maltings, turn right on a signposted track. *If you visit the Maltings, there's a footpath along the back of the buildings that joins this track further down.* Stay on this path all the way back to the picnic site.

WALK 5

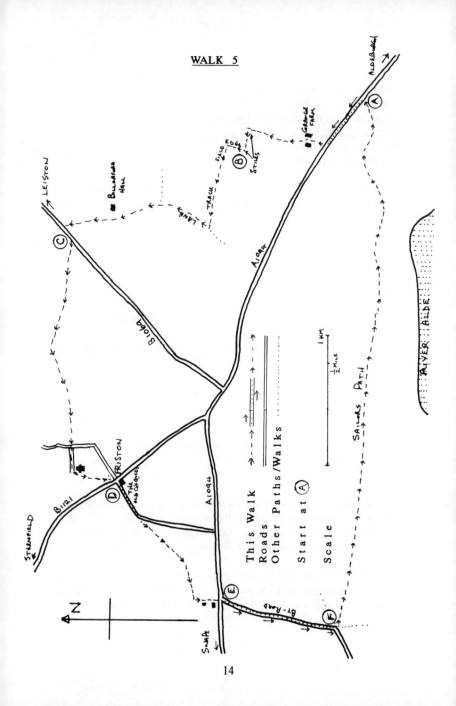

This Walk →-→-→
Roads ═══════
Other Paths/Walks ··········

Start at Ⓐ

Scale

14

Walk 5

Distance: 12km (7½m) 2½ - 3½ hours
Start Point: Aldeburgh Road (GR 442582)
Route: Friston and the Sailors' Path
Pub: The Old Chequers, Friston
Car Parking: Approaching from Aldeburgh, small car park 800m (½m)
after the golf club, on left hand side
Bus Routes: 99a, 99b, 189

A: From the car park, walk up towards Snape for about 400m, then turn right on a signed path along a farm road leading to Grange Farm. Shortly after passing between house and farm buildings you'll reach a new barn. Here turn left over a boarded stile and turn right into a lane. Walk up the lane, and, shortly after the end of the copse on the right, turn left across the field on a signed path, to reach a stile on the other side.

B: After crossing the stile on the far side, turn right into the corner, then left following the field edge. When you reach the next corner, go straight ahead on a good track across the field, to reach a lane in about 500m. Turn right on the lane, and stay on it to reach a road in about 1km.

C: Turn left on the road for 100m, then turn right on a good track taking you all the way into Friston, (about 2km). Go straight on past Friston church, then half left on a short road, and half left again on a footpath, towards the Old Chequers pub.

D: Go down Mill Road next to the pub. In about 300m, where the road bends left, go straight on along a signed path across a field. In 500m cross a track. and continue on the other side along a field edge for about 300m, then turn left on a track down to the main Aldeburgh Road.

E: Go straight across the main road and along the by-road on the other side. In about 1km you'll reach a sharp right hand bend.

F: At the bend you'll find a 2 signed footpaths to the left, and one straight ahead. Take the middle of these towards a red brick cottage. This track is the Sailor's Path, and is clearly signed as the Suffolk Coast Path, all the way back to the car park.

WALK 6

This Walk → – – → ⋯⋯⋯→ → – – →
Roads ═══════════
Other Paths/Walks ⋯⋯⋯⋯⋯

Start at Ⓐ

Scale

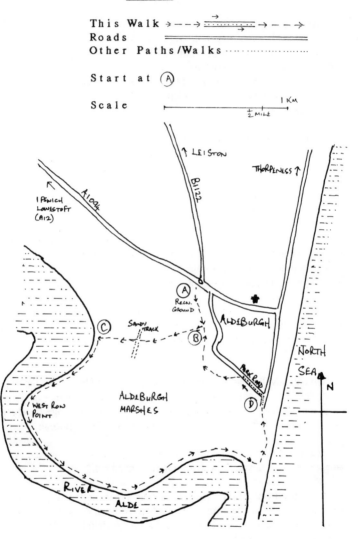

Walk 6

Distance: 6km (3½m) 1½-2 hours
Start Point: Kings Field, Aldeburgh (GR 458569)
Route: Aldeburgh Marshes, River Alde bank, West Row Point
Pub: Various in Aldeburgh
Car Parking: Playing field car park (Access from Leiston Rd Roundabout
            signed 'Fire Station')
Bus Routes: 80,81,99a,99b,126,189,563

A: Take the path across the field towards the gap in the corner between the red-brick wall and the hedge.   In about 75m look for a signposted path on the right through the allotments.

B: Take the path through the allotments, and go more or less straight on via a series of bridges and gates. In about 500m go straight on across a sandy track, to reach the river wall in about another 400m.

C: Turn left on the river wall. You'll find that you're still walking away from Aldeburgh, but at West Row Point you'll start turning back towards the town again. Continue along the wall for about another 1½km to reach a car park on the shore. Turn left on the unmade road towards the town, and walk along as far as Park Road.

D: Turn left up Park Road. In about 300m, where the road becomes a private road, take the left fork, signposted Kings Field. Continue along on the main path, soon following a red brick wall, to bring you back to the recreation ground car park.

WALK 7

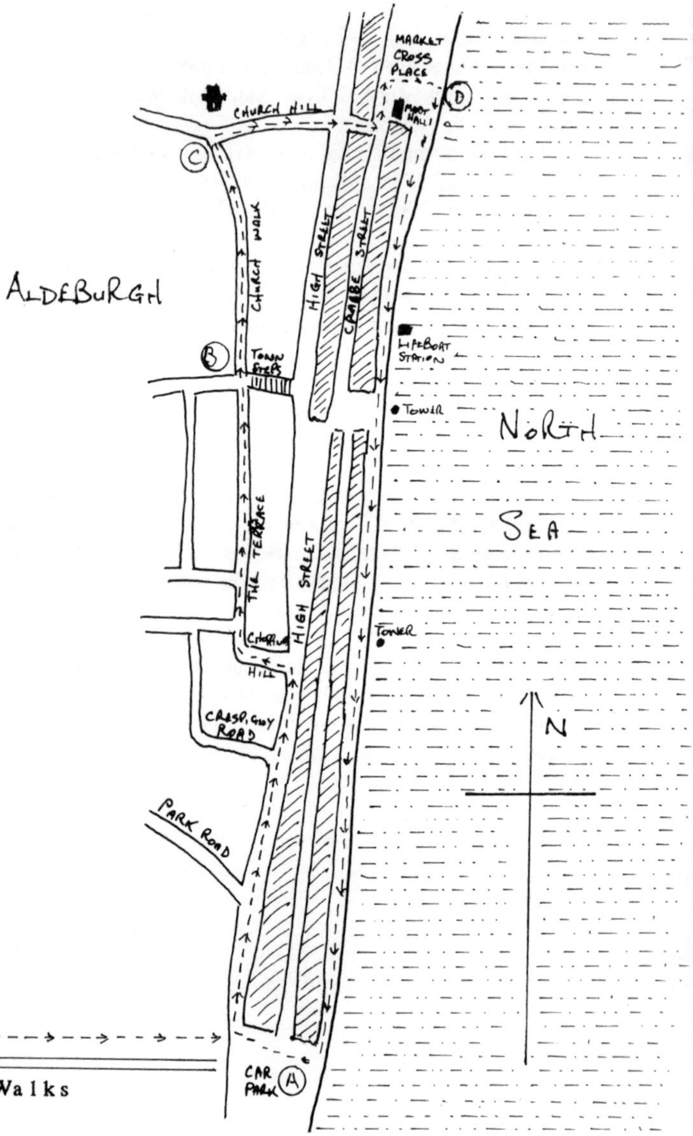
MARKET CROSS PLACE
MOOT HALL
D
CHURCH HILL
C
CHURCH WALK
HIGH STREET
CRABBE STREET
ALDEBURGH
B
TOWN STEPS
LIFEBOAT STATION
TOWER
NORTH SEA
THE TERRACE
HIGH STREET
TOWER
HILL
PARK ROAD
N
CAR PARK
A

This Walk - - → - - - → - - - → - - - → - - →
Roads
Other Paths/Walks

Start at (A)

Scale 250M

Walk 7

Distance: 2½km (1½m) ½ - 1 hour
Start Point: Aldeburgh (GR 465559)
Route: Aldeburgh Town Circular Walk
Pub: Various in Aldeburgh
Car Parking: Pay and Display car park at southern end of High Street
Bus Routes: 80,81,99a,99b,126,189,563

Please note that this is only one suggested walk round Aldeburgh, taking in just a few of the many interesting features of the town.

A: Go back along the High Street, passing several listed buildings, including the Old Custom House with its flight of stone steps. After passing Crespigny Road on the left, turn left up Chopping's Hill, taking you up to the Terrace. Follow this along, overlooking the High Street roof tops, to reach the Town Steps.

B: Continue straight on at the top of the Town Steps into Church Walk, to reach the Church of Saints Peter and Paul, the resting place of several eminent musicians.

C: Turn right down Church Hill, cross the High Street and continue on to turn left into Market Cross Place. Note the views of Thorpeness to the north, and, beyond, the massive buildings of Sizewell 'A' and 'B'. After passing the Moot Hall turn right towards the sea.

D: Turn back along the sea front. Further on you'll see this becomes the Crag Path, named after a shelly crumbly deposit found locally. After passing the lifeboat station, note the towers on the beach, built as look-out points by two rival groups of local pilots. Whilst looking at these, don't miss the tiny one roomed building on the right, called Fantasia! Continue along the Crag Path to reach the car park.

WALK 8

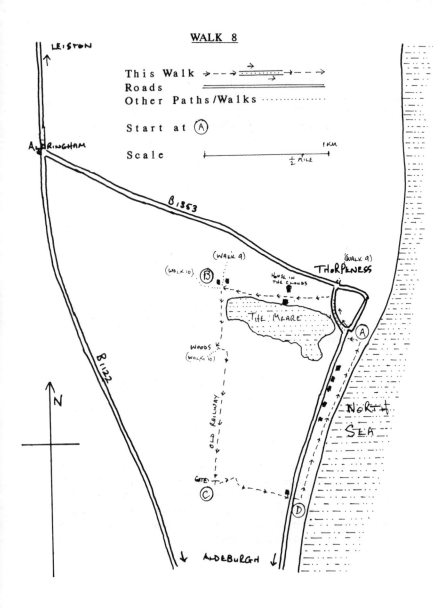

This Walk → → →
Roads
Other Paths/Walks ···········

Start at Ⓐ

Scale |————————| 1 KM
          |————| ½ MILE

LEISTON

ALDRINGHAM

B1353

(WALK 9)
THORPENESS

(WALK 9)

(WALK 10) Ⓑ

HOUSE IN THE CLOUDS

THE MEARE

Ⓐ

WOODS (WALK 10)

N

B1122

OLD RAILWAY

NORTH SEA

GATE Ⓒ

Ⓓ

↓ ALDEBURGH ↓

20

Walk 8

Distance: 6km (3½m) 1-1½ hours
Start Point: Thorpeness   (GR 472596)
Route: Thorpeness Common, Thorpeness beach
Pub: The Dolphin, Thorpeness (Badly damaged by fire in 1995)
Car Parking: Public car park near the beach
Bus Routes: 80,81,99a,99b,126,189,563

Thanks to my friend Alex Miller for his assistance with this walk

A: Walk along the main road past the Meare. Turn left along the unmade road signposted Thorpeness windmill, soon passing between the windmill and the House in the Clouds. Continue on past the Golf Club onto a signed path. After passing along between the Meare and the golf course you'll soon reach a group of cottages.

B: At the cross-track near the cottages, turn left on a shady path. Stay on this for about 400m, soon passing the head of Thorpeness Meare. Just after the path bends sharp right into some woodland, go through a gateway on the left onto a permissive footpath along the old railway. Continue along this pleasant grassy track to reach a metal gate in about 1km.

C: Immediately after the gateway turn left on a signed fenced footpath. Stay on this to emerge on the Thorpeness - Aldeburgh road, near a small bungalow.

D: Cross the road and walk over onto the good track along the shingle and turn left back to Thorpeness. When you reach the first of the houses, stay on the beach side. The car park is about 600m further on.

WALK 9

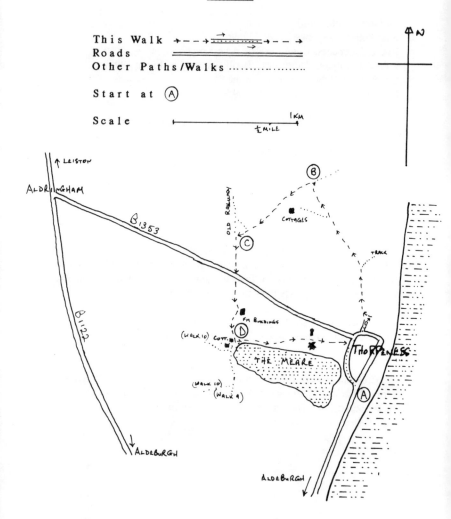

This Walk   → – → – · · · · · → – → → –
Roads
Other Paths/Walks · · · · · · · · · · · · · · · ·

Start at Ⓐ

Scale   ⊢————————— 1 KM
             ½ MILE

N

↑ LEISTON
ALDRINGHAM
B 1353
B 1122
↓ ALDEBURGH

Ⓑ
OLD RAILWAY
COTTAGES
Ⓒ
TRACK
FM BUILDINGS
Ⓓ
(WALK 10) COTT.
THE MEARE
(WALK 10)
(WALK 9)
THORPENESS
Ⓐ
ALDEBURGH

Walk 9

Distance: 4½km (3m) 1-1½ hours
Start Point: Thorpeness   (GR 472596)
Route: Aldringham Common
Pub: The Dolphin, Thorpeness (badly damaged by fire in 1995)
Car Parking: Public car park near the beach
Bus Routes: 80,81,99a,99b,126,189,563

A: Go back along the main road past the Meare. Go past the Dolphin pub, under the the almshouses arch, and along the road beyond. At the end, go right onto a track, then bear left along the back of the bungalows. Follow the signed track round to the right, soon heading more or less towards Sizewell power station.   In about 350m, the track bends to the right, and at this point bear very slightly left onto a pleasant leafy lane. Stay on this path to reach a wide and very sandy cross track in about 800m.

B: Turn left on the wide sandy track. In about 500m, where the track forks, choose the left branch, then keep left again shortly afterwards. In about another 150m you'll reach a T-junction.

C: Turn left at the T-junction and follow this wide path as far as the road in about 300m. At the road go straight across onto an unmade road. When you reach farm buildings keep right on a sunken grassy lane. Follow this to reach a cottage.

D: After the cottage turn left on a signed path. After passing along the edge of the Meare, you'll pass the golf clubhouse. Keep to the track between the House in the Clouds and Thorpeness Windmill. When you reach the road, turn right to return to the car park.

WALK 10

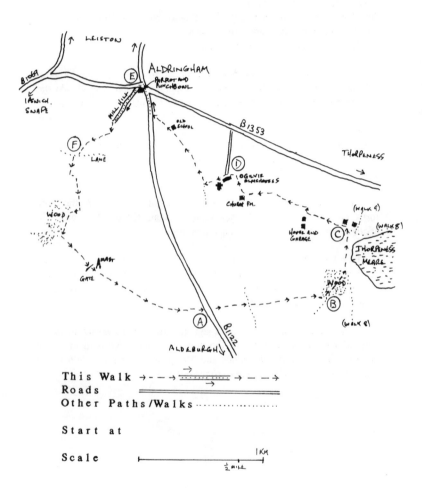

This Walk →·—·→ ┄┄┄ → — →
Roads ═══════
Other Paths/Walks ·····················

Start at

Scale ├──────────────┤ 1 KM
                ½ MILE

Walk 10

Distance: 8km (5 m) 1½-2½ hours
Start Point: Aldringham (GR 451593)
Route: North Warren Nature Reserve, Thorpeness, Aldringham
Pub: The Parrot and Punchbowl, Aldringham
Car Park: Aldeburgh-Leiston road (1½m/2½km on Leiston Road from Aldeburgh, park in wide gateway signposted Nuttery Lane)
Bus Routes: 80, 81, 126, 563

A: Go down the path opposite, signposted Thorpeness. In 400m at a cross path by a bench go straight on for another 600m to reach a T-junction.

B: Turn left at the junction, and follow the path through pleasant woods. In 250m the path bends left, and in another 150m you'll pass the head of Thorpeness Meare. Shortly afterwards you'll reach some cottages.

C: Just before the cottages, turn left on a signed path. Stay on this clear path to reach a brick garage in about 500m. Go into the corner to the right of the garage to cross a stile, then turn left up the middle of the field. At the top cross a metalled lane, then go more or less straight on. In about 200m bear right between farm buildings and continue up the track to reach the Ogilvie Almshouses.

D: Go down the road along the back of the almshouses as far as the church, then go right and immediately left down a sunken lane. Turn right at the bottom and follow the lane more or less straight on to Aldringham. Turn right on the road, and walk along as far as the crossroads.

E: Turn left by the Parrot and Punchbowl, then left again into Mill Hill in about 75m. Follow the road for 400m, continuing along the footpath at the end. After crossing a footbridge follow the line of the fence round to the right, then when the fence bends sharp left go more or less straight on to reach a lane in about 250m.

F: Turn right briefly in the lane, then left again on a signed field edge path. Keep to the field edge around several corners until you reach the wood. Turn left along the edge of the wood to reach a T-junction with a good track.. Turn left on the track and follow it through a metal gate by the radio mast. Go straight on for about 1km to reach your start point.

WALK 11

This Walk   — — —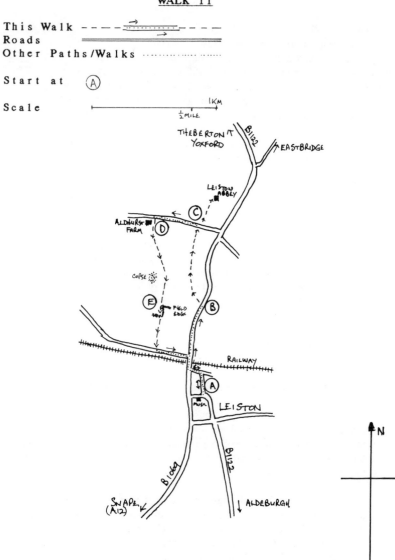
Roads
Other Paths/Walks ....

Start at   (A)

Scale

Walk 11

Distance: 4km (2½m) 1 hour approx.
Start Point: Leiston (GR 444627)
Route: Leiston Abbey
Pub: Various in Leiston
Car Parking: Park opposite Long Shop Museum in Old P.O.Square
Bus Routes: Numerous

A: Go up Dinsdale Road from Old Post Office Square. Turn left at the top to reach the main road near the level crossing. Cross the railway line, (Note the road on the left here named Westward Ho). Stay on the main road (Abbey Road) for about 450m, to a footpath on the left, signposted Leiston Abbey.

B: Turn left on the path. In about 200m follow it round the field edge as it bends half right. It soon becomes a sunken lane. After passing the next field edge, the path crosses the middle of a field to reach a narrow road (Abbey Lane). Continue up the track on the other side. When you've seen the Abbey retrace your steps to this point.

C: Turn right. (i.e. away from the main road), and walk along as far as Aldhurst Farm on the left hand side.

D: Turn left on the signed path with farm buildings on your right. When you reach the corner, go slightly left across the open field to reach a gap in the hedge. From the gap, follow the direction of the FP sign to continue up the next field (if in doubt, aim about 50m left of a copse). When you're almost level with the copse, the path bends slightly right so that you'll be heading towards the line of a hedge bordering a nursery.

E: When you reach the hedge, continue straight on into the corner. Here, go through the gap by the FP sign, and continue straight on across the nursery road, onto a path on the other side. Follow this along to the road (Westward Ho) where you should turn left to bring you back to the level crossing.

WALK 12

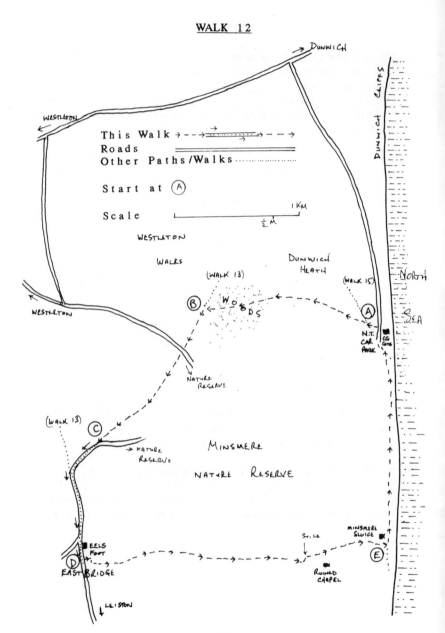

This Walk →
Roads
Other Paths/Walks ....

Start at Ⓐ

Scale ⊢————————⊣ 1 KM
                 ½ M

DUNWICH

WESTLETON

WESTLETON

WESTLETON
WALKS

DUNWICH HEATH

(WALK 13)

(WALK 15)

Ⓑ W O O D S

NORTH
SEA

Ⓐ

N.T. CAR PARK
CG GTS

NATURE RESERVE

DUNWICH
CLIFFS

(WALK 13)

Ⓒ

NATURE RESERVE

MINSMERE

NATURE RESERVE

STILE

MINSMERE SLUICE

Ⓔ

EELS FOOT

Ⓓ

EAST BRIDGE

RUINED CHAPEL

LEISTON

28

Walk 12

Distance: 8km (5 m) 1½-2½ hours
Start Point: Coastguard Cottages, Dunwich (GR 477677)
Route: North Walks, Eastbridge, Minsmere Beach
Pub: The Eels Foot, Eastbridge
Car Parking: N.T. Car Park (1995 price £1.00) - Free to members
Bus Routes: n/a

A. From the car park, go back along the access road. Just after the coastguard cottages, turn left on a signed path across the heath. Keep more or less straight on along the main path for about 700m, until it bends to the right along the edge of some woodland. Here go straight on into the wood. Follow this pleasant path for about 700m to reach a definite T-junction.

B: Turn left at the T-junction. In about 400m cross a road and continue on a grassy open path. In a further 600m this path enters woodland and descends to join the Minsmere nature reserve road.

C: Continue on in the same direction. In about 300m follow the road round to the left and in another 600m you'll pass the Eels Foot pub on the left.

D: About 100m after the Eels Foot turn left on a path signposted to Minsmere Sluice. In about 50m follow signs taking you to the right, then follow this clear path for about 2½km over a series of stiles all the way down to the sluice.

E: When you reach the red brick sluice, turn left, and follow the dune path along to the coastguard cottages in about 1½km.

WALK 13

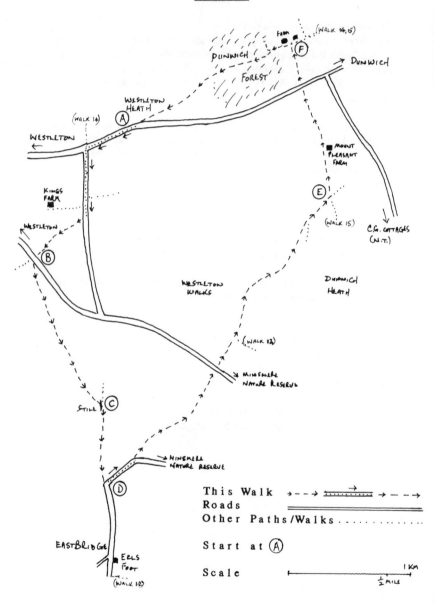

DUNWICH FOREST

FARM (WALK 14, 15)

F

DUNWICH

WESTLETON HEATH

(WALK 14)

A

WESTLETON

KINGS FARM

WESTLETON

B

MOUNT PLEASANT FARM

E

(WALK 15)

C.G. COTTAGES (N.T.)

WESTLETON WALKS

DUNWICH HEATH

(WALK 12)

MINSMERE NATURE RESERVE

STILE

C

MINSMERE NATURE RESERVE

D

EASTBRIDGE

EELS FOOT

(WALK 12)

This Walk   →‑‑→ →‑‑→

Roads

Other Paths/Walks . . . .

Start at Ⓐ

Scale   1 KM   ½ MILE

30

Walk 13

Distance: 9½km (6 m) 2-2½ hours
Start Point: Westleton Heath (GR 454695)
Route: Westleton Walks, Dunwich Heath, Westleton Heath
Pub: The Eels Foot, Eastbridge (600m off route)
Car Parking: 1km along the Dunwich road from Westleton, go straight on
onto the heath where the road bends slightly right, and park.
Bus Routes: 99a, 99b

A. Go back up the road towards Westleton, and, in about 500m, turn left on the Minsmere Nature Reserve road. About 100m after passing a gated driveway to a white farmhouse off to the right, turn right into a signposted grassy lane. In about 400m you'll reach a narrow road.

B: Cross the road and immediately turn left on a narrow signed path. Follow this improving path for 1½km to reach a stile onto a broad track.

C: Turn right on the track and follow it for about 600m to reach a metalled road. (An access road for Minsmere Nature Reserve). *The Eels Foot pub is about 600m ahead,, but if you decide to visit it, you will have to return to this point.*

D: Turn left on the road, and, where it bends right in 300m, go straight on along a bridleway. Stay on this path for 1km to reach a narrow road. Cross the road and continue on a pleasant shady path. In 400m keep straight on past a FP sign to the right. The path now continues as a broad forest ride. In about 1km the forest ride heads slightly downhill, and the path narrows. 250m further on you should reach a signposted crossways, with a broad lane ahead and to the left, and a narrow path to the right.

E: Turn left into the lane and stay on it to reach a road in about 800m, passing Mount Pleasant farm on the way. Go straight across the road, and on for about 400m on a signed path to reach a T-junction near a house.

F: Turn left at the T-junction. In about 200m where the paths fork, go left to continue on in the same direction on a wide grassy forest ride. In about 600m, you'll reach Westleton Heath. Here continue straight on to reach your car.

WALK 14

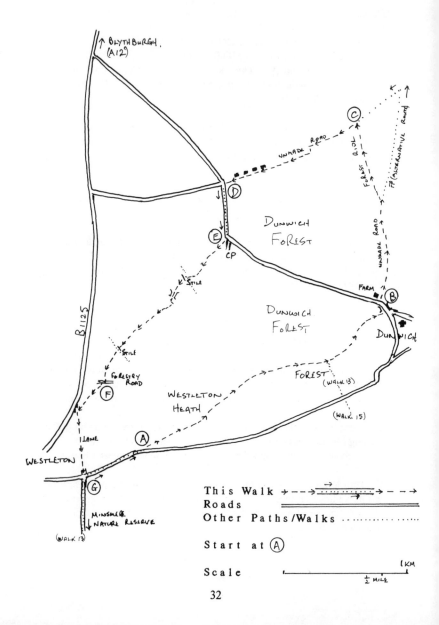

This Walk →– – –→ ··········→ →– – –→
Roads
Other Paths/Walks ················

Start at Ⓐ

Scale ├─────────────────┤ 1 KM
                      ½ MILE

32

Walk 14

Distance:	9½km (6 m) 2-2½ hours
Start Point:	Westleton Heath (GR 454695)
Route:	Westleton Heath, Dunwich, Dunwich Forest
Pub:	The Ship Inn, Dunwich (500m)
Car Parking:	1km along the Dunwich road from Westleton, go straight on onto the heath where the road bends slightly right, and park.
Bus Routes:	99a, 99b

A. Stay on the main track away from the road. Where it bends left at the forest edge, go straight on through the gateway along a grassy forest ride. In about 700m, where the paths fork, turn briefly left then right on the same line as before. In about 200m you'll pass red brick farm buildings on the left. Go straight on to emerge near Dunwich church in about 1km.

B: Turn left at the road. After crossing a bridge turn right on a good track to the right of farm buildings. Stay on it until it bends slightly right in about 700m. Here go slightly left uphill on a forest ride. (Not a public right of way - see notes in the introduction on forest access.) Continue on the ride for about 600m to reach a gateway onto a wide cross track.

C: Turn left on the cross track. After a brief 'left and right' in 400m, stay on the main track for about another 700m to reach the road.

D: At the road turn left and walk along as far as a bend in about 400m.

E: At the bend, take the signed grassy path to the right of the car park access road. Keep straight on to reach a stile in 500m. Cross the stile and go straight on downhill to cross a bridge in about 150m. Turn left briefly in a lane, then turn right along the field edge. Follow this clear path to cross another stile in about 700m. Again go straight on. In about 300m, you'll reach a T-junction with a wide forestry road.

F: At the T-junction, turn briefly right then left again on a forest track. After going slightly downhill, you'll join a sandy lane at the bottom. Turn left in the lane, and walk along to reach the road in about 500m.

G: Turn left on the road to return to Westleton Heath in about 500m.

WALK 15

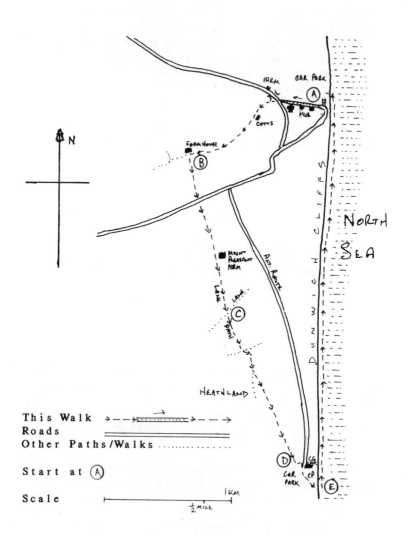

This Walk   →‒‒→▭▭▭▭→ ‒‒→
Roads   ═══════════
Other Paths/Walks ....

Start at   (A)

Scale |‒‒‒‒‒‒‒‒| 1 KM
                   ½ MILE

Walk 15

Distance: 8km (5 m) 1½-2 hours
Start Point: Beach Car Park, Dunwich (GR 479708)
Route: Dunwich Heath, Coastguard Cottages, Dunwich Beach
Pub: Ship Inn, Dunwich
Car Parking: As Above
Bus Routes: 99a,99b

A. Go back along the road, and walk up past the Ship Inn, the museum and the church. Where the road bends to the right at the top, go more or less straight on along a signposted track. In about 250m you'll pass Walnut and Apple Tree Cottages. Continue straight on the grassy path to reach a house on the right in about 500m.

B: Turn left on the track opposite the house. In about 400m cross the road and continue along the lane on the other side, signposted Mount Pleasant Farm. After passing the farm continue along the lane for another 400m until it bends sharp left at a 4-way signpost.

C: At the signpost go more or less straight on along a narrow path onto open heathland. In about 300m you'll reach a wide cross track. Turn left on the track, which immediately swings right, then left again towards the coastguard cottages. Stay on it as far as the cottages.

D: When you reach the cottages, go past the car park, and downhill to reach the shore.

E: Turn left, and walk back along the beach to Dunwich (about 3km).

A word of warning: Apart from the obvious dangers of crumbling cliffs, please be aware of dangers of very high tides. Allow at least 45 minutes to return to Dunwich along the beach. In that time, the tide can rise as much as ½ metre (2 feet), or more.

If in any doubt, an alternative is to go back along the N.T. access road, and turn right at the end to get back to the village.

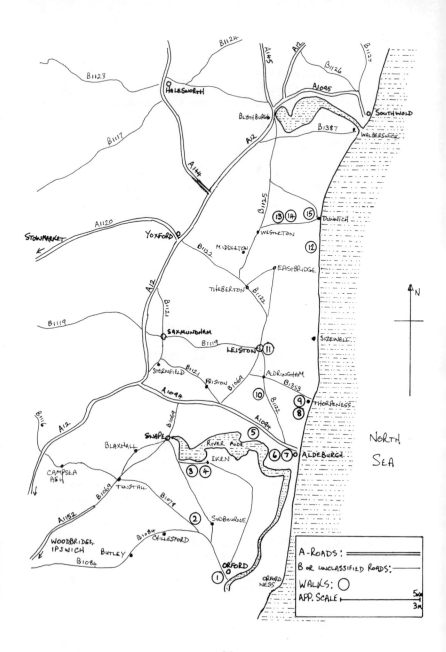

B1124
B1123
HALESWORTH
A145
A12
B1126
B1127
A1045
B1117
BLYTHBURGH
SOUTHWOLD
A12
B1387
WALBERSWICK
A144
A1120
STOWMARKET
YOXFORD
B1125
13 14 15 DUNWICH
B1122
MIDDLETON
WESTLETON
12
EASTBRIDGE
THEBERTON
B1122
A12
B1121
B1119
SAXMUNDHAM
SIZEWELL
B1119
LEISTON 11
STERNFIELD
B1121
FRISTON
B1069
ALDRINGHAM
B1353
A1094
B1069
10
B1122
9 THORPENESS
8
A12
B1116
SNAPE
5
NORTH
BLAXHALL
RIVER ALDE
IKEN
SEA
3 4
6 7 ALDEBURGH
CAMPSEA ASH
B1069
TUNSTALL
B1078
2
SUDBOURNE
A1152
B1084
CHILLESFORD
WOODBRIDGE, IPSWICH
BUTLEY
B1084
ORFORD
1
ORFORD NESS

↑ N

A-ROADS: ═══
B OR UNCLASSIFIED ROADS: ───
WALKS: ○
APP. SCALE
5km
3m